Mary Seacole

Paul Harrison

First published in 2007 by Wayland

Copyright © Wayland 2007

Wayland
338 Euston Road
London NW1 3BH

Wayland Australia
Level 17/207 Kent Street
Sydney, NSW 2000

Editor: Victoria Brooker
Designer: Jane Stanley

Harrison, Paul, 1969-
    Who was Mary Seacole?
    1. Seacole, Mary, 1805-1881 - Juvenile literature 2. Nurses
    - Jamaica - Biography - Juvenile literature 3. Crimean War,
    1853-1856 - Women - Juvenile literature
    I. Title
    610.7'3'092
ISBN 978 0 7502 5197 6

Printed in China
Wayland is a division of Hachette Children's Books, an Hachette Livre UK Company.

For permission to reproduce the following pictures, the author and publisher would like
to thank: Bettmann/Corbis: 18; Bibliotheque des Arts Decoratifs, Paris/Dagli Orti/Art
Archive:6; City of London Libraries & Guildhall Art Gallery/Heritage-Images: 17; Everett
Collection/Rex Features: 13; ©Fowokan - K.G. Kelly: 1, 19; Richard Gardner/Rex
Features: 5, 21; Guildhall Library, City of London/Bridgeman Art Library, London: 10;
Musee du Chateau de Versailles/Dagli Orti/Art Archive: 9; Nils Jorgensen/Rex Features:
4; Kathy Lockley: 20; MAPS.com/Corbis: 11; National Army Museum: 8; Private
Collection/Photo ©Christie's Images/Bridgeman Art Library, London: 12; Private
Collection/Bridgeman Art Library, London: 14; Amoret Tanner/Alamy Images: 16,
Cover; Eileen Tweedy/Art Archive: 7, 15

The website addresses (URLs) included in this book were valid at the time of going to
press. However, because of the nature of the Internet, it is possible that some addresses
may have changed, or sites may have changed or closed down since publication. While
the author and Publisher regret any inconvenience this may cause the readers, no
responsibility for any such changes can be accepted by either the author or the Publisher.

Contents

Who was Mary Seacole? 4

Mary's childhood 6

Marriage and death 8

Mary the explorer 10

Fever and war 12

At war 14

Poor but famous 16

Mary dies 18

What next? 20

Timeline 22

Glossary 23

Further information and Index 24

Words in **bold** can be found in the glossary.

Who was Mary Seacole?

Mary Seacole was a nurse. She lived from 1805 to 1881. Although a little known figure today, she was hugely popular and respected when she was alive.

The only portrait known to have been painted of Mary hangs in the National Portrait Gallery in London.

Mary became famous for her work helping British soldiers during the **Crimean War**. Her bravery in treating soldiers on the battlefield won her much love and respect.

An actress shows what Mary may have looked like during the time of the Crimean War.

Mary's childhood

Mary was born in Kingston on the island of Jamaica. Her father was a Scottish soldier and her mother was from Jamaica. Mary's mother ran a boarding house in Kingston where injured soldiers stayed.

Jamaica was an important British **colony** because it produced sugar cane. However, life for Jamaicans was harsh and there was much **poverty**.

Mary's mother was very good at curing ill people. She made traditional medicines from roots and plants. Mary learned how to help people by watching her mother.

IT'S TRUE!

When Mary was a child she enjoyed pretending to be a nurse. Her patients were her doll and any dogs or cats she could find.

Before medicines such as **antibiotics** were invented people used plants for cures.

Marriage and death

When Mary was 31 years old she married Edwin Seacole. They moved to a place in Jamaica called Black River where they set up a store. Unfortunately Edwin was not a well man, so they returned home to Kingston.

A model of Mary Seacole from the National Army Museum in London.

There was little Mary or her mother could do to help Edwin to get better and sadly he died. Mary had only been married for eight years.

IT'S TRUE!

Mary ran a hotel in Jamaica after Edwin died.

Edwin Seacole was the godson of Admiral Horatio Nelson, the famous British war **hero**.

Mary the explorer

Mary had always enjoyed visiting other countries. It was very unusual at this time for a woman to travel by herself. That didn't stop Mary, though. She went to Britain twice.

The size and noise of London was very different to Mary's Jamaica.

In 1851 she went to Panama to visit her brother. While she was there she set up her own hotel. But Mary didn't like Panama, so she gave the hotel to her brother and returned home to Jamaica.

IT'S TRUE!

While she was in Panama she helped to cure people of a terrible disease called **cholera**.

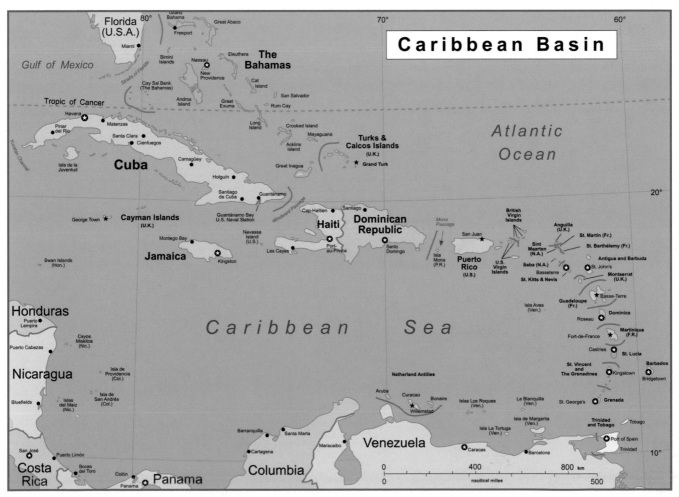

A map of the Caribbean showing both Jamaica and Panama.

Fever and war

When Mary came back to Jamaica it was gripped by a deadly disease called **yellow fever**. Mary helped to treat a lot of British soldiers who were based in Jamaica.

There had been British soldiers based in Jamaica since 1655.

The soldiers told Mary about the war that was going on in the Crimea. Mary wanted to join Florence Nightingale's nurses so she could help. She tried to join three times but was turned down.

Florence Nightingale set up hospitals that changed the way patients were cared for.

At war

Mary was determined to go to the Crimea, so she went by herself. When she got there she set up the British Hotel. This was a **boarding house**, canteen and a general store where troops could buy **supplies**.

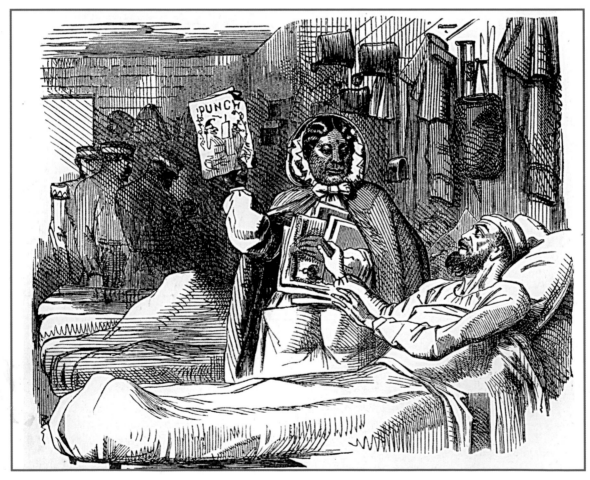

The British Hotel was very popular with the British soldiers.

Mary also nursed injured soldiers – even if that meant going onto the battlefield while the fighting was going on. Florence Nightingale, the famous British nurse, did not do this.

The soldiers admired Mary for going onto such a dangerous place as a battlefield.

Poor but famous

In 1856 the war ended suddenly. The troops went home and Mary was left with a shop full of goods that no one wanted. She practically had to give it all away and lost all of her money.

The only known photograph of Mary. It was taken on her return to London after the war.

Mary sailed to Britain and discovered she was a **hero**. The army arranged a festival to raise money for her. It lasted for four days and over 1,000 entertainers performed!

Places to Visit

Forsyth Gardens, London SE17 — all that is left of the Royal Surrey Gardens, where the festival in honour of Mary took place.

The Royal Surrey Gardens, where the festival in honour of Mary was held.

Mary dies

On her return from the Crimea, Mary met the royal family. Prince Albert even helped to organise the festival for Mary. They became friends and Mary would often meet with the Queen and Prince Albert.

Queen Victoria and Prince Albert.

After the festival Mary retired. She was in her fifties and had seen and done more than most people. She died in 1881 and was buried in St Mary's Catholic cemetery in Kensal Rise, London.

A bust of Mary Seacole from the Florence Nightingale Museum.

What next?

For many years Mary's story was nearly forgotten in Britain. However, in 1973 her grave was rediscovered and her gravestone was repaired. Slowly more people got to hear of Mary's work and in 2004 she was voted Britain's greatest black person.

HERE LIES
MARY
SEACOLE
1805 – 1881

OF KINGSTON, JAMAICA
A NOTABLE NURSE WHO CARED
FOR THE SICK AND WOUNDED IN
THE WEST INDIES, PANAMA
AND ON THE BATTLEFIELDS
OF THE CRIMEA
1854 – 1856

THIS GRAVE
A JAMA
BRITIS

VITAE CLUB
ON AND THE
FUND

Mary's grave at St Mary's Catholic cemetery, Kensal Rise, London.

Unlike Florence Nightingale there is no statue or memorial to Mary. However, an appeal has been launched to build a statue outside Guy's and St Thomas' hospital in London.

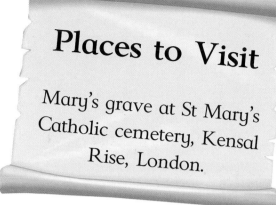

Places to Visit

Mary's grave at St Mary's Catholic cemetery, Kensal Rise, London.

Sir Trevor MacDonald opens a special exhibition about Mary at the Florence Nightingale Museum, in London.

Timeline

1805	Mary is born in Kingston, Jamaica
1836	Mary marries Edwin Seacole
1844	Mary moves to Black River, Jamaica and sets up a small store Mary returns to Kingston, Jamaica Edwin dies
1851	Mary travels to Panama
1852	Mary sets up a hotel in Panama
1853	Mary returns to Kingston, Jamaica
1854	Start of the Crimean War
1855	Mary travels to the Crimea and sets up the British Hotel
1856	End of the Crimean war Mary returns to England
1857	Mary publishes her book, *Wonderful Adventures of Mrs Seacole in Many Lands*
1881	Mary dies

Glossary

antibiotics a drug or medicine that stops germs from spreading

boarding house a place where people can rent a room to sleep in and be served meals

cholera a disease that causes sickness and diarrhoea. Severe cholera can kill people

colony a country or land owned or controlled by a different country

Crimean War a war fought between Russia and the combined armies of Britain, France, Turkey and Piedmont/Sardinia. The war lasted from 1853 to 1856

hero someone who is especially brave or does good deeds

poverty not having much money or many possessions

supplies items people need

yellow fever a disease that causes a fever and yellowing of the skin. Severe yellow fever can kill people

Further information

Books

Mary Seacole by Harriet Castor (Franklin Watts, 2001)

Mary Seacole by John Malam (Evans, 2004)

Websites

http://www.maryseacole.com
An informative website with a biography, key dates and information about the Mary Seacole statue appeal

http://www.bbc.co.uk/schools/famouspeople/standard/seacole/index.shtml
Play the object game and learn how Mary helped the soldiers during the Crimean war

Index

British Hotel 14

Crimean War 5, 13, 14, 18, 19

France 5
Florence Nightingale Museum 19, 21
Forsyth Gardens 17

Guy's and St Thomas' hospital 21

Jamaica 6, 8, 10, 11, 12

London 4, 10, 16, 20, 21

MacDonald, Trevor (Sir) 21

National Portrait Gallery 4
Nelson, Horatio (Admiral) 9
Nightingale, Florence 13, 15, 21
nurse 4, 7, 13, 15

Panama 11
Prince Albert 18

Queen Victoria 18

royal family 18
Royal Surrey Gardens 17
Russia 5

Sardinia 5
Seacole, Edward 8-9
soldiers 5, 6, 12, 13, 14, 15

Turkey 5, 13

yellow fever 12